UNICORNS UNITE

HOW NONPROFITS & FOUNDATIONS CAN
BUILD EPIC PARTNERSHIPS

JESSAMYN SHAMS-LAU
JANE LEU
VU LE

red press § england

CONTENTS

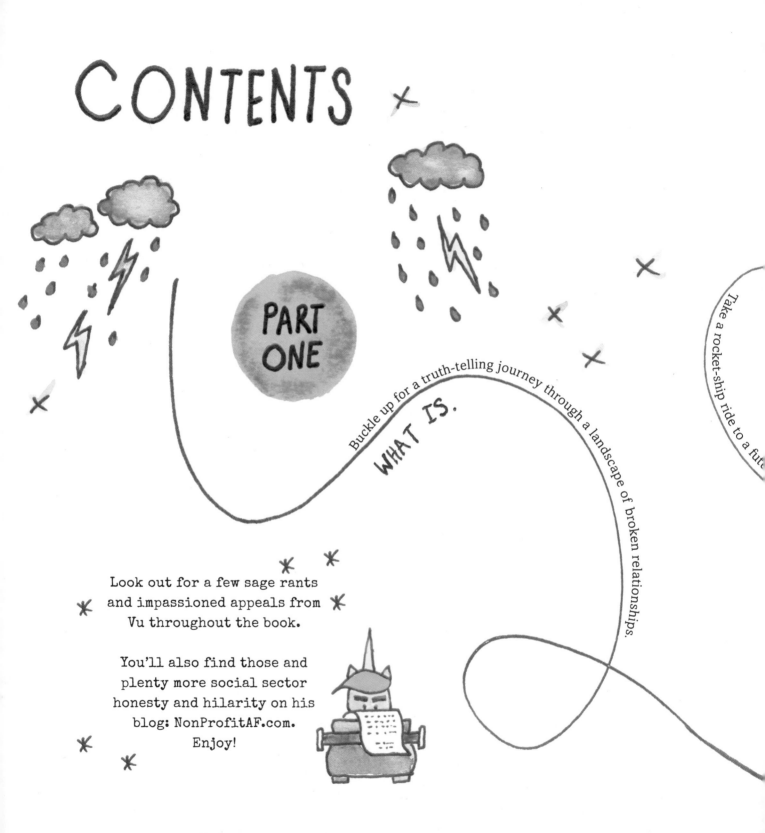

PART ONE

Buckle up for a truth-telling journey through a landscape of broken relationships.

WHAT IS.

Take a rocket-ship ride to a futu

Look out for a few sage rants and impassioned appeals from Vu throughout the book.

You'll also find those and plenty more social sector honesty and hilarity on his blog: NonProfitAF.com. Enjoy!

Dive into these fun and thought-provoking exercises. Do and discuss!

HOW TO GET THERE.

PART THREE

partnerships grounded in trust, equality and creativity.

WHAT COULD BE.

PART TWO

Dear nonprofit and foundation professionals, you are each a unicorn.

The more I work in the nonprofit sector, the more I am amazed and inspired by the people in it. You are some of the smartest people I know. You could pursue work elsewhere for much better pay and prestige—but you are here, in this sector, fighting each day to help families lift themselves up and to strengthen our communities.

You are awesome because you know that awful things in the world do not stop happening when we don't think about them. You chose this work and stick around because you believe that if we want to make the world better, we can't wait around for fate or other people to take care of things.

The work is never easy, and we put up with a lot in the quest to help end homelessness, to make elders feel less lonely, to expose kids to art and music, to make the world greener, to change unfair policies, to undo the forces of racism and homophobia and sexism and oppression, and overall to make the world better.

Thank you for all that you do. Today, take a moment to give yourself some credit.

You are a unicorn.

Love,
Vu

(NonprofitAF.com, 14 February 2014)

2

THIS BOOK IS ABOUT UNICORN UNITY

We wrote this book to invite all unicorns to talk about, and participate in, improving our sector—especially the way that we approach funding and fundraising.

We wrote this book to encourage the nonprofit sector to discuss and reject division. For too long our sector has self-segregated into two camps: funder and fundraiser; foundation and nonprofit; funding and doing.* This book offers practical steps to build one common identity and increase unicorn unity.

We wrote this book to ask unicorns to commit to being better for each other. Now more than ever, we need ways to work together that are fast, equal, and efficient. This book rejects the constraints of 'business as usual' and envisions a future of 'nonprofit as extraordinary'.

We wrote this book to welcome creativity and invite each of us to re-envision unicorn relationships: from ho-hum and serviceable (and occasionally nightmarish), to EPIC Partnerships that defeat injustice and inequality, and that unleash bold and hopeful solutions and leaders.

Most of all, we wrote this book because we admire you. You are a unique, mythical, magical, hard-working unicorn, and we wrote this book for you.

---

* We know that foundations are also nonprofits, and that not all funders are foundations, and that not all social change organizations are nonprofits—but we struggled to come up with a term that easily distinguished between organizations that make the grants and those that seek the grants. For the purposes of this book, foundations are 'grantmakers' and 'funders' and nonprofits are 'grantseekers' and 'doers'.

HOW TO USE THIS BOOK:

PART ONE

Part One is about *What Is.*

Clear your calendar, open your mind, and buckle up for a bumpy ride through a truth-telling journey about the current state of unicorn affairs: the nitty-gritty, inside, real deal on how foundations and nonprofits relate today; the root causes of our challenges; and why we need to improve. Read, reflect, agree, disagree, discuss.

PART TWO

Part Two is about *What Could Be.*

Board a rocket ship for a ride into the future where EPIC Partnerships – grounded in equality, trust, and creativity – reign. Where nonprofits and foundations join together in amazing feats that slay the dragons of injustice and inequality. Read these dreams. Dream your own dreams. Write them down. Draw them in color. Share your dreams with a colleague, a partner, your team. Live into the possibility of a future of EPIC Partnerships between foundations and nonprofits.

PART THREE

Part Three is about *How to Get There.*

Sign up to advance unicorn unity and pave the way to EPIC Partnerships. Roll up your sleeves and dive into a series of simple and thought-provoking exercises for you to do and discuss with your team, your partners, and your board. Take the insights from this workbook into your next grantmaking and fundraising cycles and emerge with partnerships that start to look more EPIC. Share your success to inspire more unicorns and more EPIC-ness.

Some of these things may be hard to hear. Please don't take them personally. Some of these things may not apply to you or your experience. Please get curious about them. Some of these things are overly-generalized. Please read for the point.

Everything in this book comes from real live unicorns and their experiences. There's no fiction here.*

* Very intentionally, there's also no academic research, double-blind randomized control trials, or literature reviews here. Other nonprofit sector books have that covered.

PART ONE

WHAT IS.

ARE **YOU** A UNICORN?

UNICORN

noun | u-ni-corn

1) A mythical animal typically depicted with the body and head of a horse with a single horn in the middle of the forehead.

2) A persistent, visionary, and dedicated nonprofit or foundation professional who shines with brilliance and practices humility.

WE ARE

Jane is a social entrepreneur unicorn, and the CEO and Founder of Smarter Good. She is obsessed with problems and their solutions, likes to build and help others build organizations from scratch, and does the fundraising needed to make that happen.

Vu is a vegan unicorn, the Writer of Nonprofit AF and Executive Director of Rainier Valley Corps. He champions equity, leads organizations, writes grant proposals, and makes us all LOL when he speaks and writes the truth about the quirky nonprofit sector.

Jessamyn is a philanthropy unicorn and the Executive Director of the Peery Foundation. She puts grantees at the center, likes taking risks in life and grant-making, and encourages other funders to do the same.

Jane and Jessamyn met in a funding partnership and found themselves spending a lot of time talking to each other about the power and privilege inside nonprofit sector relationships. Vu spends a lot of time talking about power and privilege in the nonprofit sector to the 40,000 readers of his blog, NonprofitAF.com. We teamed up to invite everyone in the nonprofit sector to join us in the conversation.

THE UNICORN FAMILY TREE

The Unicorn Family Tree has deep roots and many branches. It includes brilliant human beings who work in the public, private, and nonprofit sectors as leaders, doers, fundraisers, funders, investors, donors, volunteers, entrepreneurs, activists, organizers, researchers, and changemakers of all kinds.

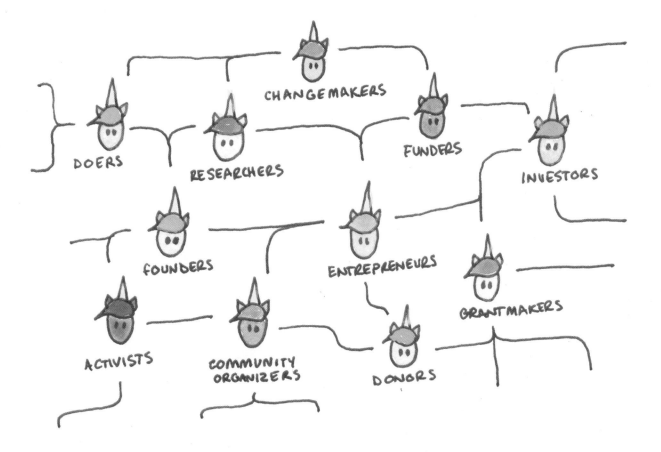

We may each have a different mission statement, but we are connected by our shared goal to create a better world. If you are reading this book, you are in the family.

7 reasons why the Unicorn Family rocks

1. We are bad-ass people:

Nonprofit work is difficult AF, with all the overhead BS and the clueless public looking down on us, to name a few. It takes a certain type of bad-ass to do it. That's you.

2. We provide jobs and strengthen the economy:

We are the third largest sector, employ ten percent of the workforce, and we contribute $900 billion to the US economy every year.

3. We handle stuff no one wants to do:

Our work fills the gaps that government and the private sector can't. We're there to make sure that none of our neighbors gets left behind.

4. We restore and build community:

With so many forces trying to tear families apart, we do the work needed to build and restore community.

5. We amplify voices that aren't heard:

We amplify the voices of people who feel like they can't speak up, or won't be listened to when they do.

6. We stand defiantly against injustice:

In a time of mass deportations and hateful marches, we mobilize to challenge bigotry and hatred in all its forms. We educate, we change laws, we protect people.

7. We bring hope:

Hope, in a time of fear, is hard to hold on to. And hope, like community, is not usually an outcome included in our logic models or theories of change, but this is one of the most important things we do as a sector.

(NonprofitAF.com, 17 November 2017)

OUR FAMILY HAS ISSUES

There is so much to love about our Unicorn Family. Yet, as in any family, our Unicorn Family dynamics can be a bit dysfunctional.

We get distracted and pull apart from one another because of

DISTRUST   JEALOUSY

POWER IMBALANCE   FEAR

HYPOCRISY   DISRESPECT

TIME-WASTING

LACK OF

LISTENING & HONESTY

Instead of banding together as peers and partners united in vision and purpose, we let our differences divide us and slow down progress.

And when it comes to money (who has it and who needs it) our family is at its absolute  WORST.

14

LET'S TALK ABOUT IT

We need to talk about our family dysfunction.

This conversation is long overdue, and we're willing to get it going, as long as you promise to join in.

Please be warned that this conversation will be awkward and uncomfortable for everyone, as we speak truth into the dark corners of our family and shine a light on each unicorn's special brand of disappointing behavior.

And yet, we come to this conversation with deep love and respect for our Unicorn Family, a belief in our potential for greatness. We also bring both a willingness to laugh at our warts and a commitment to work to fix them.

TOP 10 WAYS OUR UNICORN

Our family can act in ways that are disheartening,

NONPROFITS:

1. We trash-talk other nonprofits and bad-mouth foundations.
2. We are defensive when given feedback and ignore good advice.
3. We believe (and act like) we are entitled to funds.
4. We say what we think foundations want to hear, whether it's true or not.
5. We are not transparent with foundations about our challenges, setbacks, and needs.
6. We don't follow grant guidelines and waste time and money by applying for grants that don't fit.
7. We take funding rejections personally.
8. We act like martyrs and perpetuate a scarcity mentality.
9. We have an inferiority complex in relation to foundations.
10. We revert to 'funding pitch mode' too frequently.

FAMILY DISAPPOINTS

discouraging, and downright uncool.

FOUNDATIONS:

1. We trash-talk other foundations and bad-mouth nonprofits.
2. We give advice without understanding the context and don't seek advice from nonprofits.
3. We don't trust nonprofits to spend money where they see that it's most needed.
4. We are not clear on what we do/don't fund and rarely fund for more than one year at a time.
5. We have longer decision cycles than it takes to conceive and give birth to a baby.
6. We ask for extensive individualized info and evaluation for small amounts of money.
7. We let personal interests drive foundation strategies and set grant priorities without community and nonprofit input.
8. We punish nonprofits for having too much money in reserve.
9. We have a superiority complex in relation to nonprofits.
10. We exclude nonprofits from foundation gatherings because we don't want them to pitch us.

(For more ways in which we all disappoint, go to NonprofitAF.com and look up the GRAVE Gauge and the FLAIL Scale.)

OUR PARTNERSHIPS
NEED IMPROVEMENT

We have the raw ingredients for excellent partnerships in our sector, because the individuals in it are outstanding. Our institutions, nonprofits, and foundations are organized around inspiring shared missions, which means we have more that unites than divides us. But we have a tendency to typecast and pigeonhole members of the Unicorn Family because of the institutions they work for. This leads to ho-hum relationships that are transactional in nature, instead of being transformational for solution-making.

FOUNDATIONS ARE OFTEN FUNDER-CENTRIC.
NONPROFITS ARE OFTEN NONPROFIT-CENTRIC.
WE ARE ALL OFTEN EGOCENTRIC.

We tend to put each other into boxes labeled 'foundation' or 'nonprofit', perpetuating myths that:

- Foundation people act in unpredictable individualized ways, make arbitrary decisions and aren't responsive, think their time is more valuable than that of nonprofits, and feel they have the right to call all the shots.
- Nonprofit people act in ways that are highly transactional, only care about getting more money, over-promise and under-deliver, take everything personally, and don't know how to manage their organizations well or efficiently.

These little boxes we have put each other into have turned into big nightmares, stressing out nonprofit and foundation professionals, and thwarting our ability to work together as peers and partners in producing epic amounts of social good.

The fact is: we spend too much time and energy categorizing and criticizing each other as if we were adversaries—instead of family and close and treasured colleagues. We need to be channeling all of that energy into fighting the *real* enemies: poverty, inequality, and injustice.

IN OUR NIGHTMARES...

When we asked colleagues to share the situations that stress them out and keep them up at night, they told us about these recurring nightmares...

FOUNDATIONS SET THE TERMS & CALL ALL THE SHOTS

One funder said we were in line for a $500k grant and then ran us through the grinder during their due diligence. We spent 60 hours completing an excel sheet that required massive amounts of calculations and projections in their specific format.

60 hours?!?

The funder was in another time zone and planned calls at the end of our day, when we were exhausted and not sharp. They'd been funding us for years, but they still didn't trust us, and seemed intent on finding red flags where none existed. Every call, they reminded us how much money they'd given us, the risk they were taking on us, and that their funding was a high percentage of our budget.

Seriously?

The funder decided our staff count and salaries were bloated compared to other orgs, but when we countered with comparative data, they would not respond. They even asked us to let go of some staff and replace them with lower-paid staff.

Then what happened?

After all that, they made a grant of only $100k—saying they wanted to 'send us a message' about our deficiencies. The process was incredibly frustrating, nerve-racking, and demoralizing for our team.

Another nonprofit friend told us about a nightmare when a nonprofit partner of hers took on the role of funder:

We partnered with an international nonprofit, as 'subcontractors' of a grant they were administering for a large foundation. We had high hopes for the partnership to produce huge results because they are a star in our space. But, we soon figured out that our values weren't aligned.

But they were in it for impact, right?

We were curious about outcomes; they wanted only to see activities. They didn't care about increasing incomes for unemployed youth; they just wanted to hit their attendance target. They insisted on boosting numbers by paying training participants to attend; it was a mess. People came for the money, and had no interest in what we had to teach.

Did it get better?

Nope. During our grant period, the funding NGO went through a change of leadership, and when I met the new program lead, her first words to me were "What am I paying you to do?" She then proceeded to ask me rapid-fire questions about our organization, and myself, without reciprocating with anything about herself. It was clear that the relationship was transactional and she considered herself superior for being on the donor side.

NONPROFITS MAKE IT ALL PERSONAL

A foundation friend shared a recurring nightmare:

I did everything that I could to respect this one nonprofit director's time. I went to their location and met on a day convenient to him. I asked for documents he had already created for other funders. It was clear early on that we wouldn't be a good fit for each other, so I let him know right away.

How did he take it?

I got a very angry email back. He accused me of leading him 'up the garden path'. He said that his organization's work would halt and dissolve solely because of our decision to not provide funds.

How often does this happen?

Often! Even though we take care to be clear and transparent, nonprofits don't always understand that our board sets the priorities, not us program officers. Nonprofits take those rejections very personally when they aren't personal at all. And they get so focused on money only. That organization didn't dissolve without a grant from us—quite the contrary.

One foundation friend shared with us:

Sometimes we meet founders or nonprofit directors who clearly have ego issues. There's a palpable sense that the whole thing is set up to be a show in which they are the star, instead of meeting needs of community or mission. One nonprofit we met with presented himself as the savior of the organization. He was more interested in using the organization as a vehicle for his own success, and showed zero passion or commitment for the work. It was simply a way for him to play the hero.

WE STRUGGLE TO BE IN THE SAME ROOM TOGETHER AS PEERS

Several foundation friends shared a common nightmare with nonprofits:

It had been a really long day at a conference overseas. I was still jet-lagged, and had done about 12 meetings in a row with nonprofit and foundation partners. It was 10pm and I was at the cocktail party, having a drink with a friend and colleague who was asking me how things were going with a family member who had been ill. A nonprofit executive busted into the conversation and started to give me his pitch. Normally I'm very open to hearing about people's work, but there is a time and place for everything, and that wasn't it.

I invited another nonprofit director to join a panel about trends and emerging issues in our work. The audience was mixed, but mostly foundations. We had done a prep call to outline some of the key challenges in our field and to structure how he could link what he's seeing from both the ground and landscape level to help shape the strategy of funders in the field. But when it came time for the panel, he spoke only about his organization, giving an unabashed pitch for their work, instead of giving his landscape view on how the field could work together to create better results. I felt burned.

Several nonprofit friends told us that this nightmare happens all the time:

I was at conference for foundations; my foundation partner invited me because she felt my expertise would add value to the conversation. In the conference folder the first thing I saw was a notice in big letters: *This is a no-pitch zone. Under no circumstances can nonprofits talk about their work or pitch the foundations present.* But there was no statement asking foundations not to evaluate the work of nonprofits they met that day.

And foundation friends shared their dismay that this happens too:

As part of my work for a foundation, I attended a round-table on re-designing a major international innovation fund to be more responsive to nonprofits' needs. There were no nonprofits invited, only funders.

And for this unicorn friend, she hadn't even had her coffee yet when this nightmare happened in broad daylight:

As an exhibitor at a foundation conference, we had paid a substantial amount of money to participate, which helped to defray some costs for foundation attendees, so they could have a great experience and learn a lot. I grabbed some breakfast from the buffet and pulled up a chair at a table near my booth and introduced myself to the woman already sitting there. She asked, "What foundation are you with?" I said, "I'm not. I'm an exhibitor here." She literally turned her back and did not utter another word to me.

SADLY, 10/10 UNICORNS

HAVE EXPERIENCED
SUCH NIGHTMARES

AND TO MAKE MATTERS WORSE...

Society makes us all feel insecure.

Both foundation and nonprofit friends tell us that our career choice can be a nightmare to explain to people outside the sector.

President, scientist, firefighter, astronaut, doctor, lawyer, artist, athlete, teacher... As with other jobs, it's not easy to find *one* word that perfectly describes what we do, and we're reminded of that fact every time we need to fill in the box marked 'profession' on a form.

Society rarely depicts our collective work as the stuff of childhood dreams. Parents rarely envision our careers as a successful outcome of their blood, sweat, and tuition support. Most of our family and friends still don't know exactly what we do. Many people assume that we are volunteers, and are surprised to learn that we are actually paid for our work.

Many nonprofit and foundation professionals – especially those of us from immigrant and refugee backgrounds, and who are first-generation college grads – have to contend with challenges within our own families, in addition to those we face from society. Besides the misconceptions or complete lack of understanding of what we do, there is also the nightmare of constant comparisons to others with more 'successful' and 'prestigious' careers. We have feelings of guilt for letting our families down or not being able to support them financially, being attacked by the communities we are trying to help, and existential doubts about our place in our families and our worth to our communities.

It's complicated and troubling that our important and critical work lacks a professional identity, and that it is a recurring nightmare to deal with how society sees us.

How to deal with your family who has no idea what a nonprofit is or what the heck you do

In choosing this path, many of us will feel the guilt of letting down our families. I started college as a pre-med student, aiming for psychiatry, and I dropped it to go into social work. The disappointment from my parents was something that stuck with me my entire career. They had gone through so much – a war, reeducation camp, refugee camp, the giving up on their dreams so we kids could have a future – and the least I could do was become a doctor instead of being so selfish in pursuing this career. It would have made them so happy...

The guilt also comes in other forms. A major one involves not being able to support your family financially. Says a colleague: "I can say that the hardest part of working in this space is not being able to financially support or contribute to my family as my sister has done (she's a CPA). I do what I can to help my parents, but I live in the Bay Area and it's just so expensive. I'm always reminded by my mom of how much I can't financially help them or treat them. She's been asking me to buy her a car, and that's just unrealistic."

(NonprofitAF.com, 5 September 2017)

THE WORLD NEEDS NIGHTMARE-FREE UNICORNS

We love our work in the nonprofit sector but hate the nightmares that keep cropping up and distract us from the important work we all do.

WE'RE STUCK.

A big reason why we are so stuck is that we are all a bit afraid to name, and then address, the root causes that create division in our sector.

Here's our analysis of the root causes:

$$\$ \quad \text{MONEY}$$
$$\times \quad \text{TRUST}$$
$$\neq \quad \text{STANDARDS}$$

33

WHOSE

$ MONEY

IS IT

?

Once a person or a group places their wealth into a foundation, it is no longer theirs. It no longer belongs to individuals or families. It doesn't belong to staff or boards or corporations or nonprofits.

NOBODY owns the money in a foundation. It belongs to the foundation, which is also not owned by anybody—not even the founder or the board.

The funds in a foundation exist to serve the **PUBLIC GOOD.**

Even if we know this is true, we all still act as if the money belongs to the foundation's donor, board, and/or staff. And:

Even if it's unconscious, Money = Power.

We assign more power to the donors or representatives of the money. A *lot* more power.

Even if it's unconscious, People With Money = Powerful People.

Power shapes interactions between boards and staff inside both foundations and nonprofits, and between staff members of nonprofits and foundations.

Power determines when and where we meet, how we talk (or don't talk) with one another, and how much we share (or don't share). Power determines who has to adhere to character counts and who can write at any length they choose. Power determines who is accessible and responsive and who is not. Power determines who gives and receives advice and feedback. Power determines who is paid for their expertise, who must give it for below-market salaries, and who must give it for free. Power determines who has the final decision, and who doesn't.

MOST
IMPORTANT

KINDA
IMPORTANT

NOT VERY
IMPORTANT

$

Creating public good and positive social sector outcomes requires many inputs. Right now there is a clear hierarchy of inputs, and money is at the top of it.

Money is prioritized as the MOST IMPORTANT input to social change, and we tend to disregard or undervalue all other inputs, such as:

leadership

labor

caring

hope

risk-taking

optimism

creativity

technology

knowledge

data

and experience

(among others).

HOPE

THE TYRANNY OF THE
HIERARCHY OF INPUTS

Stacking the inputs of social change from most to least important diminishes the importance of the PEOPLE who contribute those inputs and produce outcomes, especially people and communities most affected by injustice.

The hierarchy keeps us in our little boxes of 'money-giver' or 'money-seeker'. It means we are unable to honor and value all the contributions of the people at nonprofits and in communities, which we know extend beyond giving labor in exchange for funding. It means we are unable to honor and value all the contributions of people at foundations, which we know extend beyond giving money.

Money – its ownership, and its position at the top of hierarchy – is the number one root cause of most of our Unicorn Family dysfunction.

CAN WE
X TRUST

EACH OTHER

Trust-based grantmaking: What it is, and why it's crucial for our sector

There seems to be a pervasive lack of trust between funders and nonprofits, and it's affecting us and our ability to survive and do our work. The default relationship between funders and nonprofits is one of suspicion of the latter by the former, which leads to funders enacting policies and practices designed to make nonprofits more 'accountable', such as restricted funding, individualized applications, bespoke budget forms, customized reports, and other things that drive us nonprofits nuts. This, in turn, leads to nonprofits hiding information (especially about challenges) from funders, which in turn reinforces the suspicion. All this perpetuates a depressing cycle of waste of time and energy (and lots of complaining, usually at bars), all of which could have been used to deliver programs and services.

Funders and nonprofits are most effective when the relationship starts with trust, not suspicion. The default right now is one of mistrust: *Is this organization legit? Does it have its 501(c)(3)? Are its staff even qualified? Will it spend my money properly? Will it do what it says it will do? Does it even know what it's doing? Will it embarrass my foundation?* All these concerns are often unconscious, and are very similar to the concerns that society has about poor people. They also lead to the ineffective and frustrating practices that, on a daily basis, make nonprofit professionals want to abandon civilization to live in a van down by the river.

(NonprofitAF.com, 24 October 2016)

Nonprofits distrust foundations, doubting their seriousness, motives, and ability to truly understand grantees' work and day-to-day challenges.

Nonprofits distrust other nonprofits, viewing them as competitors and losing sleep that they might beat them out for grants. And so nonprofits don't team up.

I DON'T TRUST YOUR MOTIVES OR UNDERSTANDING

I DON'T TRUST YOU WITH MY FUNDERS

DIAGRAM OF DISTRUST

I DON'T TRUST YOUR DUE DILIGENCE

I DON'T TRUST YOU TO SPEND MONEY WISELY

Foundations distrust other foundations' judgment, feeling that they don't do enough (or the right) due diligence on their grantees. And so foundations don't team up.

Foundations distrust nonprofits, worrying that they will waste their money or spend it on the wrong things and make them look bad.

At the root of our dysfunction is a lack of trust. A web of distrust surrounds the nonprofit sector. It clouds our relationships and manifests itself in ways of working that keep us divided.

However, trust rarely gets named out loud as an issue.

Instead, foundations talk of 'risk' and the 'need to manage risk' as code for conveying a lack of trust in nonprofit organizations. And so grants get restricted, or funds are only committed for short periods of time.

Nonprofit professionals don't trust foundations to appreciate, or be comfortable with, the high level of financial risk they take personally and professionally to start, grow and sustain organizations. While they worry about the risk of not being able to make payroll for employees, failing so spectacularly that funders will not give one more dollar (and having to eat cat food in retirement), they are conditioned to hide these risks to instill funder confidence and trust. And so there's too much over-promising of results, and too little transparency about challenges and needs.

Foundations and nonprofits distrust communities, not trusting them to share their needs, or create and implement their own solutions, and demanding that they share personal information and data to prove that they qualify for services. And so community voices and needs aren't always prioritized as much as they should be.

Communities distrust foundations and nonprofits, doubtful that the latest 'innovative program' will work, and dubious that they will stay around after the money is spent. Communities have little power to talk about risk, but bear daily risk to trust and participate in programs and services that promise a new future even when past programs may not have delivered results.

42

Take risks. Faster.

Take risks and accept failure. And do it faster.

If Dr. Martin Luther King Jr. were alive today and he said "I have a dream..." the likely response from so many funders would be: "Your dream is great. But where's your data? Do you have a track record? How do we know this will work? Where's your logic model? How will you sustain this 'dream' after our support runs out? How do you align with our strategies? Is your dream scalable? Why don't you write this proposal and we'll get back to you in nine months?"

We cannot achieve equity if we do not accept risk and failure. Injustice is complex. If it were simple, we would have ended it already. It's not, so we have to be willing to try different things, and accept that not everything we try will succeed.

And we must do it all much faster.

(NonprofitAF.com, 21 February 2017)

WHAT DOUBLE

≠ STANDARDS

?

We've got two sets of standards in our field: one for foundations, and one for nonprofits.

These divergent standards typically favor foundations, but not always:

We expect nonprofits to meet strict deadlines for grant request submissions.
We expect foundations will formulate and communicate grant decisions whenever they are ready.

We expect nonprofits to pay their staff as little as possible to keep costs down.
We expect foundations to pay their staff a good, though not necessarily competitive, salary.

We do not expect nonprofits to have reserves, and if they have one, we often question whether they truly need any more money.
We expect foundations to keep huge reserves to enable them to operate in perpetuity, or to their chosen time horizon.

We expect nonprofits to provide profuse gratitude to foundations.
We expect foundations to graciously receive gratitude from nonprofits.

We expect nonprofits to provide as much of their time and information as asked for by foundations.
We expect foundations to protect as much of their time and privacy as they want.

We expect nonprofits to set clear guidelines who they will and will not serve, and this is perceived as them being 'focused', rather than 'not caring about the community'.
We expect foundations to fund as many organizations as possible, and when they don't we accuse them of 'not caring about the community'.

We need to stop treating nonprofits the way society treats poor people

The punishment of success. Ironically, while we expect poor people to work and save up money so they can stop being dependent—we punish them when they succeed, removing their benefits if they earn close to an amount where they may actually be able to no longer need the benefits. It's paradoxical, demotivating, and insulting.

In nonprofits, many funders expect sustainability and yet punish nonprofits for having a strong reserve, which is probably the most important factor for sustainability. *You need to be sustainable, but if you are too successful at that, we're not funding you, or we take away the money we gave you.* I remember frantically trying to spend some leftover money because it otherwise would have had to be returned, per the requirement of this funder, even though the reason we had leftover was because we were spending it wisely; that money we saved would have greatly helped our programs if we had been allowed to put it into reserve.

The expectation of gratitude. Every single time I bring up some sort of feedback regarding ineffective, time-wasting funding practices in our sector - such as requiring board chair signatures on grant applications (Why? Whyyyyy?!) - inevitably some people say: "People are giving you their hard-earned money, and you're whining? You should just be grateful and comply." It's the same as poor people being expected to just be happy and appreciative of whatever scraps they manage to get. Not that we shouldn't be grateful, but gratitude should not be one-sided, and it should not prevent the exchange of feedback.

(NonprofitAF.com, 18 July 2016)

WELL THAT'S
DEPRESSING.

You may be feeling that too much divides us.

Not true. **There is more that unites us than divides us.**

Let's look at what we can all agree upon:

1. The world's problems are big, hairy, and complicated.
2. These problems will not fix themselves.
3. We are the ones who can fix these problems, and we're committed to doing it.
4. Our commitment makes us unicorns!

Compared to the problems outside, the problems we have inside the Unicorn Family are minor. Tiny, even.

These problems are infinitely fixable. At the root. It will take hard work, but unicorns have never shied away from hard work.

Before we start the hard work of fixing ourselves and our partnerships, let's envision a future in which that work is in motion, and our partnerships start to be as aspirational and inspirational as our collective hopes for a better world.

PART TWO

WHAT COULD BE.

HOW TO USE PART TWO

If you can dream it, you can do it. Unicorns are good at making dreams – of equality, opportunity, security, and prosperity – into reality. Part Two is about getting clear on our dreams for our own sector.

It's about starting with the end in mind.

In this part, you'll get to read about the dreams of some other unicorns. Use these as inspiration to create your own dream for a partnership that would transform your work. Dream daringly of things unseen. Build a picture of the future that's out-of-this-world yet tangible; practical yet beautiful.

Read our dream of EPIC Partnerships. Think about how EPIC Partnership might change your unicorn relationships. Get excited by the Unicorn Manifesto. Join us. And sign on!

ONE DAY SOON...

Foundations and nonprofits recognize each other as smart, dazzling, visionary unicorns who want to build beautiful vibrant communities and enrich the planet.

Nonprofits and foundations excel at building peer relationships based on equality, respect, trust, shared standards, and common (bolder!) goals.

We do whatever it takes to help each other thrive and, as a result, everyone thrives.

We asked our nonprofit and foundation colleagues to share their dreams for our sector, and then we took those dreams one step further to imagine how those dreams might look once put into practice.

If we can envision it, we can create it.

DREAM STATE:

FOUNDATIONS & NONPROFITS PRIORITIZE NEEDS AND WORK AS EQUALS AND TEAMMATES

A nonprofit friend shared her dream:

> Foundations award six- and seven-figure multi-year general operating support—and instead of paying for line-item expenses in our budget, they pay for the outcomes that our collective organizations want to achieve. Nonprofits are seen as more than just the service providers, but as actual thought partners whose insights and experiences drive foundations' goals and inform strategies for systems-level change.

For years, we have ALL been saying we want to achieve that dream.

Put into practice, it could look like this:

Allison and Alonzo sit on the floor, shoes off, surrounded by sticky notes and markers. Allison's chef is in the kitchen whipping up lunch while Alonzo's toddler plays quietly with a stuffed animal in a porta-crib nearby. Allison grabs a flipchart sheet and starts sketching out the number of communities that the organization could potentially benefit over the next three years.

Alonzo cracks up. "Seriously, Al? You know it took us ten years to get to deep and meaningful results in this state, we're going to get to three states in thirty-six months?"

"You're right. That's ridiculous. What impactful growth could we pull off in the next three years?"

Alonzo grabs a green pen and starts sketching out the infrastructure they could build that would get them to the point where three states in three years would be easy to achieve. He starts by increasing each staff salary by fifty percent. Allison marks it up by another ten percent.

"What about if we pull in some other nonprofits too? There are some really good ones working on this same issue and their ideas will make this better," Alonzo mused.

"Great idea, we can also pull in some other foundations, too." Allison added. They sit back on their heels and look at what they've drawn.

"That is awesome! Let's do it!" they say in unison, laughing. After ten years of working together to eradicate poverty in their community, they often finish each other's sentences.

Allison whips out her phone and wires $1M over to Alonzo's nonprofit organization (with a cc: to her foundation board of trustees), while Alonzo hops on his team's virtual message board to get the plan into action.

DREAM STATE:
FOUNDATIONS & NONPROFITS PRACTICE RADICAL HONESTY AND EMPATHY

A foundation friend shared her dream:

We are honest with one another.
We each share what keeps us up at night.
We each share what gives us joy.
We explain what makes us love our work, and what makes us
dread starting another workweek.
We feel empathy for each other's unique challenges.

The way we might get there could look like this:

It's 10pm and after brushing her teeth, Brittany – a Program Director at a nonprofit – starts her bedtime ritual. She picks up her phone and hits 'record' to start a new voice note.

"Cash flow, that's still a problem. The XYZ Foundation said we'd get our grant check in July, but it's already September. I didn't take a paycheck last week because I don't know when that grant might arrive. We lost another great candidate we wanted to hire because the salary wasn't high enough and we don't do 401K contributions.

"Audit prep. *Blegh.* Where to start? Our board member who usually helps with accounting questions is in South Africa and not available and I have no idea how to fill out some of those spreadsheets. I feel annoyed that our organization has to spend $10,000 on an annual audit when we need that money to pay people. The only reason we are doing it is for the funders, but then it increases our overhead percentage and funders don't like that.

"We got a form rejection from an invited proposal that took my team 10 hours to write. Colossal waste of time and it made me feel disrespected. On a high note, our new program is really taking off and the community responded positively to it. Our software system is finally implemented and we saved 5 hours of staff time this week because of the automated reports, and that made the team happy to be able to put their efforts elsewhere.

"And… our program manager got accepted into a top grad school—and while we have to replace her, I'm proud of her and glad we could help her onto this career path."

She hit 'stop', saved the recording with the date, and uploaded the file to the Unicorn Empathy Project, which would distribute it to foundation professionals in the morning.

Truth be told, Brittany felt silly and a bit whiny doing these nightly recordings, but she noticed that she was sleeping better because she had said out loud and honestly the things that made her proud about her work—and those that cause her anxiety and take away from the joy in her job, a job she loves, loves, *loves*.

In the morning, she would download and listen to the recording made last night by her Unicorn Empathy Project partner, Bashir, a Program Officer of a major private foundation. Even though they had never met, she could empathize with the time and effort that he put into his board packet, and his frustration when he discovered that not one of the board members read it before the meeting.

At first she was surprised to hear that Bashir often felt powerless when he spent a lot of time educating his board on the issues that nonprofits are trying to solve and they still rejected his recommendations, but now she recognized it as a theme. She also could feel Bashir's pain in having to say 'no' to grant applicants; she felt the same way turning away people they couldn't serve. She identified with his joy when another foundation started to use his due diligence format because they thought it was so well done. She also wished that there was more of a career path for Bashir at his current foundation. It was clear from the recordings that he would have to look for a new role if he wanted to keep building his career.

Listening to Bashir's recordings helped Brittany to adjust her expectations of her foundation partners, and she found herself respecting and trusting them more, and interacting differently with them.

At the end of the year, all of the participants in the Unicorn Empathy Project plan to come together and re-design the nonprofit sector to reduce stress and anxiety and increase impact. Until then, Brittany and Bashir trust that their honest sharing of joys and challenges will lead to better outcomes overall.

DREAM STATE:
FOUNDATIONS & NONPROFITS LIVE BY THE GOLDEN RULE

Both nonprofit and foundation friends shared with us their own version of this dream:

> Foundations and nonprofits treat each other as they wish to be treated. They only give advice when they are willing to accept it. They scrutinize each other's strategies, results, and finances. They value each other's time equally, not asking for things they won't read, not writing things they wouldn't want to read themselves, scheduling meetings that are at times and locations convenient to both, setting timelines that are respectful of each other's urgency and work-loads.

WHAT WORKS FOR YOU?

WHAT WORKS FOR BOTH OF US?

It could look like this:

Cecilia works at a foundation that has signed on to the principles of
Golden Rule Partnership, a practice advocated by The Global Committee of Funders,
a leading philanthropy association. The practice is based on the Golden Rule,
which holds that people should do unto each other as they would have done to them.

One of the core practices of Golden Rule Partnership is that no foundation should launch a new grant proposal application until they try to answer the questions for their own foundation. Conversely, no nonprofit should submit a grant proposal application until they can summarize it in one paragraph, the way the program officer will present it to the foundation board.

Cecilia's fingers fly across the keyboard as she tackles the first question on her
foundation's grant proposal: 'Describe your program activities.' The answer comes easily as
she reflects on what she does, day by day, at the foundation. The next question stumps her.
'What is your theory of change?' Good question. *What is* their theory of change!?
Her board never talks about it, and she's unsure if they even *have* one.
The next question is even harder: 'How do you measure impact?' She wonders: is it
dollars granted? No—that would be an output, not an outcome, and certainly
would not qualify as sustainable impact. She scribbles some notes
to bring up with the CEO, and schedules a meeting with her for the next day.

Cecilia is grateful that her foundation is committed to Golden Rule partnerships.
Her foundation even did away with reporting from grantees after trying to complete
one of their own report templates and discovering how much time and
effort it took. Instead, the foundation's grantees now submit materials in
the format of a board presentation. She's seen how the simplicity of
the Golden Rule has resulted in better relationships,
less wasted time, and better impact
for their program areas.

DREAM STATE:

NONPROFITS & FOUNDATIONS DESIGN COORDINATED MOVEMENTS OF SOCIAL CHANGE

As nonprofit and foundation unicorns, we – the authors – dream of reimagining the way that we work together toward social change. Of dispensing with the habits and norms that don't serve the communities we work with well. Of expanding our current definitions of 'collaboration' and 'partnership'. Of setting aside our egos and our insecurities to become more than the sum of our parts.

One day, it'll all be like this:

It's Global Change Day. Bashir wakes up and rushes to a nearby sports stadium, where he and some of his Education for All teammates will present their Global Change Report to a group of 10,000 young people—half of whom will join virtually from all around the globe.

He starts his talk by explaining a bit of ancient history. "Before you were born, there were two primary types of organizations whose job it was to solve social issues – called nonprofits and foundations – and most of them were pretty small. Each would produce its own report to summarize its results every year—called an 'annual report'. The tricky thing was that a citizen would have to read hundreds, maybe thousands, of these annual reports to understand whether a particular social issue was improving or not."

"Those annual reports were a symptom of a really big problem. There were hundreds of organizations working on the same issue, but each doing its own thing in its own way. They couldn't figure out how to work together across geographies, organizations, and issue areas—and they didn't even want to." There's an audible gasp from the audience. Bashir laughs. "I know, right? Teamwork is such a global value now, but it wasn't always."

He hits a button and Brittany appears on the screen behind him. "This is my teammate Brittany. Hey Brittany, tell them how we met."

"Hey Bashir! So, back in the old days, we were both part of an experimental project to build empathy between nonprofits and foundations—and through that, we realized that we were all too focused on our own organizations, rather than the problems we were trying to solve.

"About a hundred of us were doing that empathy project, all working at nonprofits and foundations that were improving education in some way. We each gave a copy of our annual report to an artificial intelligence firm, which produced one universal goal statement for the whole group. We always joke that it took a robot to help us humans see how much we have in common! About seventy-five of us committed to work on that goal together, and now we produce one Global Change Report on our results.

"Funny: just envisioning that we could, and would, only report as a team changed how we interacted. Conferences became real-time working sessions, ideas got sourced from everyone, and because results drove the process – not money – people felt more empowered and equal in the way they contributed their expertise, creativity, infrastructure, distribution, money, technology, optimism, and story-telling. The same goes for giving feedback—as soon as money stopped driving the process, we weren't afraid to give the kind of feedback we needed to improve what we were doing.

"The first group annual report we produced was weak. The results weren't great, but our peers appreciated the transparency, and our Education for All team gained new members and got better at working together. Our third annual report was much stronger. Our tenth one was a hundred times better than our first. Other teams, working on other issues, started to form in the same way.
And I suppose the rest is history!"

AND ONLY $\frac{1}{1,000,000}$* UNICORNS

HAVE HAD A DREAM SITUATION

* *Totally made-up statistic from our non-existent double-blind, randomized, placebo-controlled trial. But you get the point, right?*

WHAT'S YOUR DREAM STATE?

Think about the bold change that your organization wants to create in the world.

Think about a current nonprofit or foundation relationship that is fully aligned with your vision and goal.

What could make it exponentially better? How would it make you feel when it reached its dream state? What would a year in the life of that relationship look like when it was operating at its full potential?

Let your imagination go wild. Write a description of what your dream partnership could look like. Don't hold back. Think deeply about the details and aspects of the relationship that make a difference.

It doesn't have to be award-winning prose. Simply capture whatever comes to mind in paragraphs, bullets, or a sketch.

Do it now. Don't worry. The rest of the book will wait until you have your dream state so firmly in mind that you can see, taste, and feel it.

WE DREAM OF **EPIC PARTNERSHIPS** THAT **TACKLE** COMPLEX PROBLEMS & ACHIEVE **INCREDIBLE FEATS** OF SOCIAL **CHANGE** THAT ENABLE THE **WORLD** TO **THRIVE**

WHAT ARE EPIC PARTNERSHIPS?

EPIC PARTNERSHIP FRAMEWORK

E   **Equally value all inputs,** especially time and money. Partners do not allow any input to eclipse all others in importance, power, or prestige.

P   **Prioritize needs** of those we serve. Nonprofits put needs of clients, communities, and change first. Foundations put needs of nonprofits and communities first.

I   **Increase trust and empathy.** Partners identify as peers, trusted colleagues, teammates, and equals who learn from and challenge each other and the field to excel.

C   **Commit to big, bold, and better.** Partners think big, act boldly, and produce better results—through all-in teamwork.

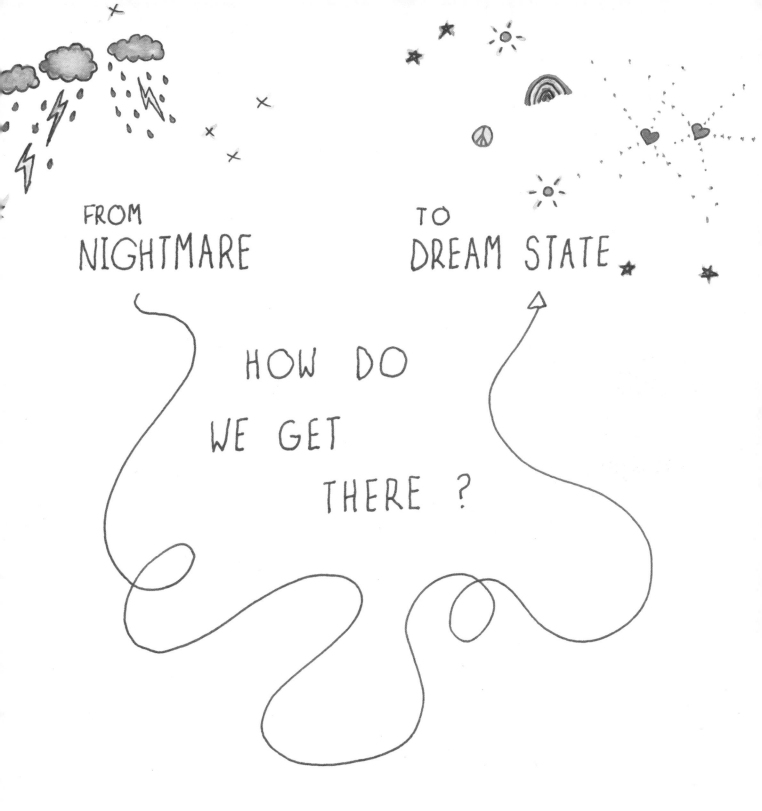

FROM
NIGHTMARE

TO
DREAM STATE

HOW DO
WE GET
THERE ?

Before we go further, let's review what we know.

We are unicorns: individuals who devote ourselves to creating change for communities and the planet. We are all members of the same family.

Sometimes our family can be dysfunctional, and this dysfunction causes nightmares— the kind that are real and happen frequently in everyday life. But we are talking about it now and getting it out in the open.

We're stuck, but now we know why.

Money, trust, and standards are at the root of our dysfunction, and perpetuate practices and policies that reek of inequality, create artificial divisions between nonprofits and foundations, and limit the quality of our partnerships to 'just okay'.

We can see and envision a dream state, with EPIC Partnerships and incredible results. And now that we see it, we want that dream state.

So let's get it. Together.

THE
UNICORN
MANIFESTO

WE ARE UNICORNS

WE DREAM

YOUR NAME: _____

SIGNATURE: _____

WE EQUALLY VALUE ALL INPUTS

PRIORITIZE NEEDS of THOSE WE SERVE

INCREASE TRUST AND EMPATHY

COMMIT TO BIG, BOLD, AND BETTER

74

OF **EPIC** PARTNERSHIPS BETWEEN NONPROFITS & FOUNDATIONS THAT TACKLE *complex problems* & ACHIEVE *INCREDIBLE FEATS* OF SOCIAL CHANGE THAT ENABLE the WORLD TO THRIVE through ALL-IN TEAMWORK

BEFORE YOU GO
ANY FURTHER

Sign

THE MANIFESTO*

* Make your commitment public by signing up on our Facebook page! (Find us at facebook.com/UnicrnsUnite, and don't forget to drop the 'o'!)

WHILE WE MAY BE A MAGICAL GROUP...

…we will not achieve a dream state by magic.

This is going to take work.

Work on ourselves;
work on our nonprofits;
work on our foundations;
work on our partnerships.

Turn the page, and get started.

PART THREE

HOW TO GET THERE.

HOW TO USE PART THREE

Part Three is where you get to put the Unicorn Manifesto into action!

There are four practices in this section, each with quick and easy exercises designed to point you in the direction of EPIC-ness. We've marked each exercise with who it's for.

Nonprofits, look for this symbol: Foundations, here's yours:

Start anywhere. Read the exercises. Pick one that looks fun and get started. Skip around. Write in the book. Draw in it. Plan in it. Rip out a page and hand it to a colleague to do the exercise together. Focus on the topics that resonate. Don't get stuck on the validity of those that don't.

Don't overthink it.

There is no right way to do these exercises. They aren't scientifically-proven methods. There's no academic framework to this. Human relationships are varied, complex, and messy. It's not about perfection. It's about building lived experience. Just try one, and spend twenty minutes walking in another unicorn's really awesome shoes.

EQUALIZE THE VALUE OF INPUTS

These exercises look at how we value and efficiently deploy the various inputs to social change, including time, advice, expertise, contacts, creativity, and others.

SMASH THE INPUT HIERARCHY

No one likes an overheadhole: the nonprofit that pretends that every dollar goes to programs and not one penny goes to overhead. It's not true. It perpetuates the hierarchy of money. It also gives the false impression that people and their salaries, facilities, electricity, and technology are not important inputs to results—and we know that they are.

Use this exercise to audit your communications, and to cut out or replace language that reinforces the overhead myth.* Check off each box once you've completed editing that communication channel. Start with the ones we've listed, and then add other documents or publications of your own. Smash the input hierarchy and build trust with nonprofit peers, too!

WEBSITE

PROPOSAL
TEMPLATE

REPORTING
TEMPLATE

ANNUAL
REPORT

"... every $ of your donation funds the people, resources, & facilities that enable us to..."

* For more on this particular topic, head to overheadmyth.com.

SAVE TIME

At some point, most foundations have said something along the lines of: "We received over 1,000 applications to our request for proposals, of which we selected 10 nonprofits to provide grants to." It's time to change that narrative, and the inefficient practice that drives it.

While it's important to be open to new ideas, nonprofits, and approaches—is the mountain of accumulated hours that unsuccessful nonprofits devote to your application process really worth it? Perhaps there's a better way to allocate your time, and theirs.

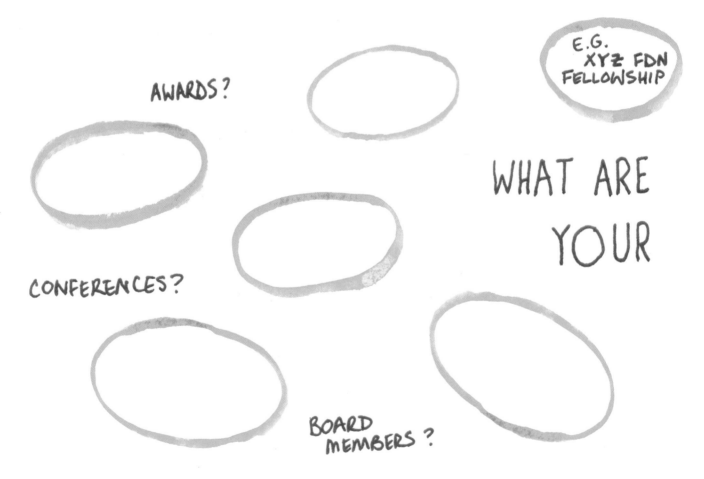

Discuss with your team what a low-time method of remaining open to new nonprofits could look like (it can be as simple as someone who picks up the phone!). Then spend the majority of your pipeline time deliberately searching for and cultivating nonprofit relationships that you are highly likely to be a fit for. Consider diversity, equity, and inclusion as you do.

Fill in the spaces below by answering these questions:
- Where do you currently find your best pipeline?
- What sources have you not tried that look promising?
- Where might you find excellent nonprofits that have fewer established networks and connections?

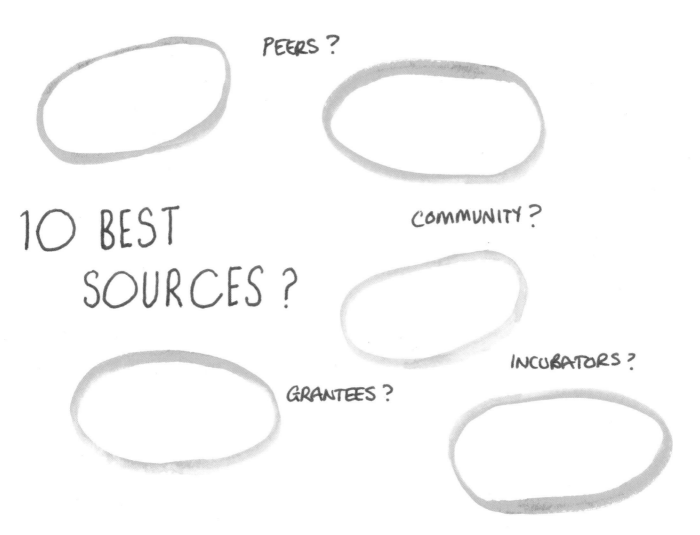

REDUCE DUE DILIGENCE TIME

We're all curious (and want to know the answers to everything), but if you ask only for the information you'll actually use to make a decision, we'll all save time.

Assess whether your due diligence process takes the amount of time that you think it does. Is it appropriate for each grant size? You need less information than you think. Use this exercise to consider what is absolutely essential to reaching a recommendation or grant decision.

Your most common grant size:

What's the ideal amount of time that your staff should be spending to make a recommendation for a grant of this size? How many hours would you ideally say that nonprofit staff should be spending on their proposal and/or due diligence? Now give your best guess for how long your process currently takes. Finally, ask 3–4 grantees to track or estimate how long the process actually took them (but bear in mind they are likely to underestimate and/or underreport).

	IDEAL	GUESS	ACTUAL
FOUNDATION HOURS			
NONPROFIT HOURS			

If there's a big disparity between your ideal and actual numbers—go through a recent due diligence document. Highlight (or ask your board to highlight) what points were actually discussed as part of the decision-making process. Distinguish between interesting, useful, and essential information.

REDUCE REPORTING TIME

Nonprofits spend countless hours every year formatting, reformatting, and shoehorning their information into foundation-required reporting guidelines. Some foundations ask nonprofits for materials prepared for internal use or for other foundations.

Use this exercise to evaluate that practice for your foundation.

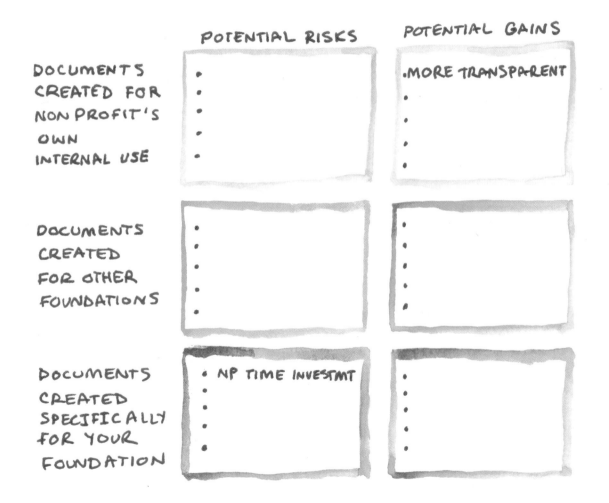

	POTENTIAL RISKS	POTENTIAL GAINS
DOCUMENTS CREATED FOR NONPROFIT'S OWN INTERNAL USE	• • • • •	• MORE TRANSPARENT • • • •
DOCUMENTS CREATED FOR OTHER FOUNDATIONS	• • • • •	• • • • •
DOCUMENTS CREATED SPECIFICALLY FOR YOUR FOUNDATION	• NP TIME INVESTMT • • • •	• • • • •

ALIGN TIME

FDN

Reporting is rarely simple, and is the black hole of nonprofit time. It's not that nonprofits don't want to report on their work—they do, but when they have to report differently internally vs. externally, and differently from one foundation to another, it becomes an extraordinarily complex and yet repetitive process. Do you know what it actually entails to complete your foundation's reporting process?

Complete your own reporting process. ☑   How long did it take you?   _____ HOURS

How long does it take your grantees to do it?   _____ HOURS

Now that you know what it takes to complete your own reporting process, think about what aspects of it are essential. How can your reporting process align with reporting activities, timelines, and methods a nonprofit is already committed to?

HOW CAN YOU IMPROVE IT?

1. ALIGN REPORTING/SITE VISITS W/OTHER FUNDERS OR INTERNAL REPORT CYCLES.

2. USE NONPROFIT'S OWN INTERNAL MILESTONES INSTEAD OF SETTING FOR THEM.

3.

4.

5.

6.

VALUE INPUTS BEYOND $

Resources other than money – like technology, a dedicated and healthy workforce, or local government and business connections – are also inputs that drive social change. Everyone is looking for resources, and good partners always share resources. This exercise makes a game out of driving resources toward each other. Nonprofits take the lead by introducing the idea to their foundation partners.

Invite your funders to a game of BOLO (Be On the Look Out) Bingo. Provide them with bingo cards of your organization's needs. Start with the suggestions below and fill in the blanks, or create your own from scratch. Ask funders to create a BOLO Bingo card with their own needs. These could be introductions and contacts needed, qualified recommendations, etc.

BE ON THE LOOK OUT BINGO

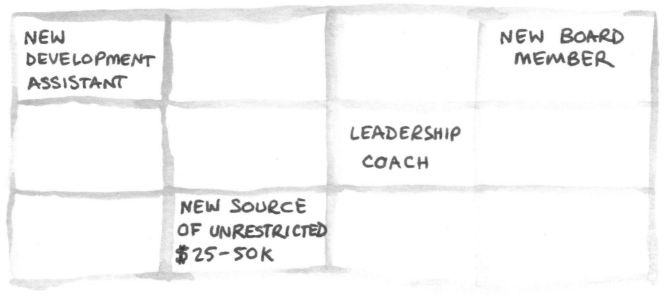

The first one to bingo wins! And so does social justice!

VALUE TIME

Nonprofits and foundations can benefit from having a common way to value time, so neither partner's time gets over- or under-valued.

This exercise puts a real dollar value on every hour required to raise a nonprofit's entire budget each year.

Typically a nonprofit executive director (ED) spends at least 50 percent of their time on fundraising each year. By dividing the organization's total fundraising goal by hours available to fundraise, we arrive at the opportunity cost of the ED's time. In other words, we're figuring out how much the director must raise with each hour that they devote to fundraising.

Illustration:
- Nonprofit annual budget: $1,500,000
- Hours ED can spend on fundraising: 1,040 hours (which is half of a 2,080-hour year)
- ED Fundraising Opportunity Cost per hour (FOC = annual budget/hours): $1,442

NONPROFIT ANNUAL BUDGET: $ _____

HOURS ED SPENDS FUNDRAISING: _____ HRS

ED FUNDRAISING OPPORTUNITY
COST PER HOUR (FOC) = $\dfrac{\text{BUDGET}}{\text{HOURS}}$: $ _____

Nonprofits:

Use this exercise to decide how best to invest your Executive Director's time. Utilize resources such as Grant Advisor and peer advice to estimate how many hours a grant application/due diligence process may take you, and what the likely grant size will be. Divide the likely grant size by the estimated number of hours it takes to apply. This number should be equal to, or greater than, your FOC (calculated on the previous page) for it to make sense for your ED to put time into it. For larger nonprofits, you can also use this calculation to estimate your development team's FOC per hour to determine which grants to prioritize and how much time to allocate to them.

Foundations:

Use this opportunity cost number to make decisions about where to ask grantees to invest their Executive Director's time in your grantmaking process and relationship.* When you calculate the opportunity cost per your grant size, does it seem appropriate?

Illustration:
- ED Fundraising Opportunity Cost (FOC): $1,442
- Hours to complete grant process: 15
- Cost to nonprofit = hours x FOC: $21,630

So, the grant size should be greater than $21,630 for it to make sense for this ED to spend 15 hours on it!

HOURS TO COMPLETE GRANT PROCESS : [HRS]

COST TO NONPROFIT = HOURS * FOC : [$]

≥ TO GRANT SIZE ? ☐

Bonus points for considering your foundation's other expectations/requests for nonprofit ED time during a grant cycle (e.g.: attending foundation events or providing issue area expertise).

PRIORITIZE NEEDS AND TAKE RISKS

These activities are designed to build empathy and understanding of needs, create awareness of those areas where you might not be focused on the needs of those you serve, and determine how to face – together with your partners – the risks that your work involves.

ASK FOR WHAT YOU NEED

NP

General, unsolicited advice from foundations flows as freely as cheap wine at a fundraising event—and similarly, it can give nonprofits a big headache. Ask foundation partners to redirect their advice-giving energy toward being on the lookout for the specific resources and contacts that your nonprofit needs.

Write a sample script for the ideal start of a relationship with a foundation. Channel bravery to bring up your desire for resources instead of advice. This will help foundations to prioritize your nonprofit's real needs.

Here's one script to get you started. Then write your own below, using one need from your BOLO Bingo square on page 87.

Funder:	What ways can we help your organization other than funding?
Nonprofit:	I'm all covered with advice and consulting, but I really need people to be on the lookout for us.
Funder:	On the lookout how?
Nonprofit:	Generally on the lookout for resources, or powerful ways to advance our mission. Right now, we are specifically looking for a contact within the Department of Justice. Do you think anyone on your team or board might have networks to help us find one?
Funder:	We can look into that!

YOU: _____

FUNDER: _____

YOU: _____

FUNDER: _____

YOU: _____

FUNDER: _____

YOUR NEEDS – THEIR NEEDS

You have criteria that determine which nonprofits are the best fit for your foundation.* List the high-level items of your criteria.

Now put yourself in the shoes of the Executive Director of one of the nonprofits you fund. What criteria would you use to determine which foundations would be the best fit for your needs, and worth the time to work with? Take a stab at creating a nonprofit hypothetical criteria list. Are there expectations on that list that your foundation could address to make it easier for nonprofits to work with you?

YOUR CRITERIA

1.
2.
3.
4.
5.

THEIR CRITERIA

1.
2.
3.
4.
5.

* Bonus points for listing your criteria and priorities on your website!

LOOK FOR WHAT YOU NEED

Selection goes both ways. If your nonprofit had criteria to determine what foundations would be the best fit for your needs, what would those look like? Take a stab at creating your criteria. Envision the foundation partners that do and don't meet your guidelines. Pay particular attention to any deal-breakers on the list.

1.

2.

3.

4.

5.

6.

NUDGE YOUR NEEDS

Nonprofits need to ask for what they need. That means making requests that are awkward and uncomfortable. Still, you need to ask, be quiet, and let the foundation respond. Over time, as all nonprofits ask for what they need, these questions become expected and standard practice.

The Golden Silence is the moment after you ask a question. Before your next foundation partner phone call or meeting, role-play asking the questions below with your colleagues. Get comfortable with the uncomfortable silence that follows.

Nonprofit: Would you consider making that $50k grant general operating support?

Nonprofit: Thank you for the $50k unrestricted grant! Would you consider committing the same for next year, and the year after?

And it's okay to hear a 'no' after a Golden Silence. When you do, don't argue the point. Take that 'no' and move on. But if you don't ask—it's always going to be 'no', even when it might have been a 'yes'.

ASK RISKY QUESTIONS

Nonprofits are equally responsible for shaping EPIC Partnerships. How might you take more risk to ask for what your organization needs and wants to deliver on your mission? Which foundation is most likely to genuinely consider your requests? Which program officer might you take risks with first?*

✓

☐ 1. Write a list of the polite requests you'd like to make of foundations. Make them.
    Eg: The guidelines say you only fund projects. Would you consider funding general operating support?

☐ 2. Create a list of points to negotiate for your next grant cycle. Negotiate.
    Eg: 1x a year report instead of 4x a year; phone meeting not grant proposal at renewal; no site visit, come to regular program event instead.

☐ 3. Write a list of questions you have of foundations. Ask them with an open and curious mind.
    Eg: Why does your foundation feel like it needs to change strategies and program areas so frequently?

☐ 4. Write a list of questions you have for your program officers. Look for ways to be a better colleague and partner.
    Eg: What's your next career step and how can I help you achieve it?

* If your initial interactions are awkward and uncomfortable, you are doing it right. It gets better the more we all take risks.

THE FIRST & FOREMOST, PRIMARY, ESSENTIAL, NUMBER ONE NEED

Nonprofits talk nonstop about their need for general operating support. It enables them to make long-term decisions, respond swiftly to changing environments, and sleep at night because they can provide multi-year commitments to their staff and communities. Some foundations, however, want to see exactly where their money is spent.

This empathy-building exercise can help your foundation team or board to understand why unrestricted funding is the number one need for nonprofits.

Imagine that you are the head chef at the Dusty Apron Gluten-Free Organic Bakery. A group of friends pooled their money together to buy a cake for their professor's 50th wedding anniversary.

To make the cake, here is what you need: 4 eggs, 3 sticks of butter, 2 cups of sugar, 3 cups of flour, 1 vanilla bean, 3 cups of chocolate chips, and some electricity.

Here are the costs:
- Eggs: $1 each
- Flour: $1 per cup
- Sugar: $1.50 per cup
- Butter: $2 per stick
- Vanilla: $2 per bean
- Chocolate: $1 per cup
- Electricity for the oven: $2 per cake

However, the friends each have specific restrictions on how they want their money to be spent:

- Jamal will pay up to $7, but his money cannot be used for eggs or electricity, and he will pay for no more than 1 stick of butter.
- Baz will pay up to $6, but his money can be used only for chocolate or vanilla.
- Sofia will pay up to $5, but her money can only be used to buy eggs, sugar, or butter, and not the full amount of any ingredient.
- Ali will contribute up to $4, which can be used to pay for anything except chocolate.
- Kat will contribute up to $5, and will pay for anything except flour, but only if another person contributes an equal amount.

Figure out how much everyone will be paying for what part of the cake.*

	EGGS	FLOUR	BUTTER	VANILLA	CHOC	SUGAR	ELEC	TOTAL
JAMAL								
BAZ								
SOFIA								
ALI								
KAT								

It's not really the point, but if you want to see the right answer, head to our Facebook page (facebook.com/UnicrnsUnite)

ANTICIPATE UNKNOWN NEEDS

General operating support is the best way to meet nonprofit needs. (See previous exercises, and every article written by a nonprofit leader, ever.)

If, for some reason, your foundation can't provide general operating support, this exercise helps you to consider providing contingency funding in addition to grants tied to a project budget.

Pick a project grant you recently made, and ask yourself: what could possibly go wrong?!? Use your knowledge, experience, and imagination to fill in the diagram.

PROJECT/GRANT: _____
EVERYTHING THAT **COULD** GO WRONG...

E.G. KEY STAFF MEMBER LEAVES

Was it hard to anticipate the unknown? How might explicitly providing contingency funding help your grantees as they navigate the unknowable? Reflect on and discuss how your foundation can support your partners' needs that are unknown at the time of the grant.

PUT CLIENT NEEDS FIRST

NP

Nonprofits complain about the forms and process foundations require to access grants and their lack of trust in nonprofits. Do we turn around and impose on the community's time and privacy in similar ways?

Fill out all the forms your nonprofit requires of the people you serve. ☑

Now do it in a second language.* ☐

At a team meeting, discuss how to revise your process to put client needs first and increase trust, respect, and empathy. What information is absolutely necessary (perhaps due to government requirements), and what information is potentially useful but not essential? How can you make the forms and process easier for clients whose first language is not English?

HOW CAN YOU IMPROVE YOUR FORMS?

1.

2.

3.

4.

5.

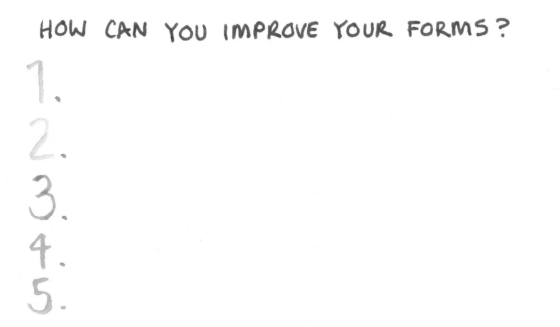

Did you fill it out in a second language? If not, maybe there's a lesson in that decision...

INCREASE TRUST, RESPECT, AND EMPATHY

These exercises can help to surface ideas on ways to make more decisions based on trust, demonstrate respect in our interactions, and create practices and policies that are empathetic to each partner's needs and context.

HIRE EMPATHY

If you lack first-hand experience in building and running the types of organizations that your foundation supports, then hire staff that can fill those knowledge gaps for you. This includes finding folks with fundraising and donor reporting know-how. Think about the other kinds of insights that a person who has worked for the type of organizations you fund could bring to your foundation. Consider how that diversity of experience and perspective might influence the way that you address equity and inclusion in your work.

Select those who know the game and the risks involved, but also know where rules can be altered—and who aren't afraid to do so!

IN WHICH POSITIONS WOULD THIS BE USEFUL?

HOW WOULD YOU ARTICULATE THIS IN A JOB DESCRIPTION?

WHAT ARE 3 INTERVIEW QUESTIONS THAT WOULD IDENTIFY THIS?

IDENTIFY POWER DYNAMICS

"The best definition of privilege I've heard is anything you don't have to wrestle with, that you don't have to think about." – BROTHER ALI, RAPPER

That's the tricky thing about power and privilege—they exist mainly in our blind spots. Try to identify the things you rarely have to think about or consider when talking to and working with nonprofits. What ways does power show up in your interactions with nonprofits? Then list small habits that might start to shift those power imbalances. We've started you off with a few ideas. Pick one idea and do it for a month.

CARRY A NONPROFIT'S BUSINESS CARDS + LOOK FOR CHANCES TO GIVE THEM OUT	SEND HANDWRITTEN THANKYOUS AFTER MEETING WITH NONPROFITS	
ARRANGE TO DO ALL NONPROFIT MEETINGS @ OR WITHIN 5 MIN OF THEIR OFFICE		
ASK A NONPROFIT TO EDIT YOUR REJECTION LETTER		

DIG DEEPER

No one is asking anyone to have *sympathy* for unicorns who work in foundations or nonprofits. We all have some of the best jobs on the planet. We are, however, asking, imploring, and urging nonprofit unicorns to build *empathy* with foundation unicorns. And vice versa.

Come up with questions you can ask to gain more insight into the work of your funders. Ask at least one in your next foundation check-in meeting. See if you can build understanding about challenges faced and successes achieved by foundation unicorns. Enter with an open, curious mind and an empathetic heart.

1. E.G. WHAT MADE YOU GO INTO THIS WORK?

2.

3.

4.

5.

6.

7.

WHAT DOES IT TAKE ?

A simple question can be a big obstacle to EPIC Partnerships in the way that it is phrased, the statistics it needs, the calculations it demands, the character limit it expects, and the future it requires a nonprofit to predict. Unwittingly, foundations ask questions that eat up time for nonprofit professionals who feel obliged to answer them.

This exercise asks you to look at one of those questions and to diagram the process to get to an answer. Take some time to truly consider what it takes to meet your expectations. Given everything else you want them to accomplish, is this a good use of their time? Will the answer change your funding decision? Ask each person on your team to diagram a different question and discuss it at a team meeting. Compare your diagram with real life when you next meet with a grantee.

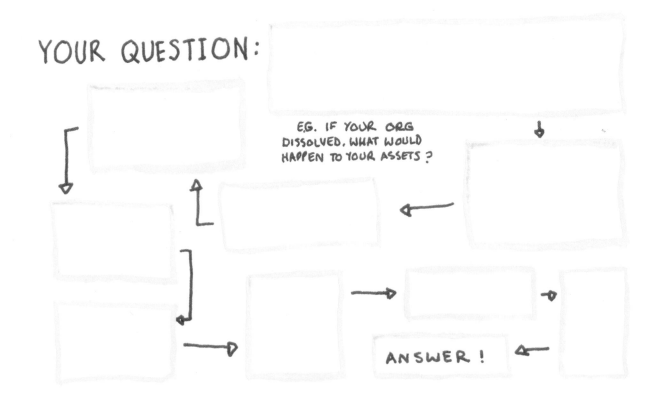

YOUR QUESTION:

E.G. IF YOUR ORG DISSOLVED, WHAT WOULD HAPPEN TO YOUR ASSETS ?

ANSWER !

Nonprofits like to see themselves as sacrificing more, working harder, and caring more than their foundation peers. Often they see themselves as the *real* unicorns, the stars and headliners of the social sector—with foundations in a supporting role at best. This builds a wall that doesn't serve us well. Foundations are unicorns too.

Let's create a united unicorn movement by building empathy. Not to be confused with sympathy.*

Sympathy:
Noun | sym·pa·thy
Feelings of pity and sorrow for someone else's misfortune.

Empathy:
Noun | em·pa·thy
The ability to understand and share the feelings of another.

Diagram what steps a program officer would have to take before presenting a grant request for your organization to their board. Think through the details. What does the full process look like? Compare your diagram with real life when you next meet with a funder.

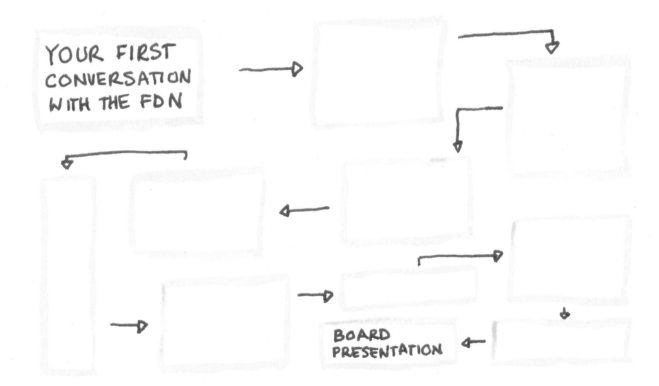

* For an excellent description of the difference, take three minutes to look at Brené Brown's RSA video on empathy.

ASK FOR TRUST

Nonprofit professionals need to build more muscle in asking for what you want—especially when what you want is general operating support. Try editing all your written communications materials so that they only mention general operating support. Ask for the trust you need!

Set a timer for 60 minutes.

Go through your website, social media, proposals, grant acknowledgment letters, and anything else you can think of.

Insert   *"GENERAL OPERATING SUPPORT"* *"CORE SUPPORT"* *"UNRESTRICTED FUNDS"*   everywhere you can.

Change "Thank you for your support" to

"Thank you for your general operating support!"

You get the idea. See how much you can edit before the timer goes off.

106

MINIMIZE THE POWER DYNAMIC

Let nonprofits know that you want to be accountable to them. Establish the expectation that your foundation is interested in hearing their input and ideas.

Ask nonprofits for their advice on your foundation's strategy and performance, their ideas on what you could do differently. Perhaps they can share power-dynamic-minimizing ideas they've seen elsewhere. It can be difficult for nonprofits to give foundations honest criticism or suggestions face-to-face, so solicit anonymous feedback on your work and approach intermittently. Regularly discuss what you hear with your team.

There are a number of tools you can use to ask for or encourage feedback from your grantees. Fill in the blank rows if you know of other tools. Use the columns to list the aspects of feedback tools that will help you identify which is right for your foundation, and then research each option so that you can fill in the full grid. Use your completed grid to kickstart a conversation with your team about instituting a feedback tool at your foundation.

	COST	TIME INVESTMENT			
GRANTEE PERCEPTION REPORT (CEP)					
GRANTADVISOR.ORG					
FUNDERFEEDBACK.ORG					
NET PROMOTER SCORE					

REINFORCE TRUST

FDN

Listen, discuss, and then DO! Once you have more information about what works and doesn't work—how will you change? Where can you grow? What changes will enable you and your nonprofit partners to achieve great feats together? Report back to nonprofits on how their input was taken seriously and changed your practice. And thank them for it! How will you hold yourself accountable for turning feedback into action? We've started you off with a few suggestions, but make sure to add more squares of your own too.

ACCOUNTABILITY BINGO

ASK GRANTEES IF SEEN IMPROVEMENT AFTER 6 MTHS	CALENDAR TIME TO GO THROUGH FEEDBACK	
	ADD GRANTEES TO ADVISORY BOARD	BLOG ABOUT WHAT YOU HEAR AND DO WITH IT
	FEATURE FEEDBACK IN ANNUAL REPORT	

BE AN ADVOCATE

One nonprofit told us that they had over 85% success rate with warm introductions, compared with less than 10% for cold introductions.

Almost all foundations love to provide value beyond their grant support. Warm funder introductions make a world of difference for nonprofits. Foundation unicorns: proactively build relationships with other foundations in the interests of your grantees. The same goes for nonprofits. When you have a great relationship with a foundation don't hide it—share it. When you see funders you know or work with that could be a good fit for brilliant peer organizations, proactively make the connection.

Use your social equity thoughtfully, but generously, when you see potential partnership opportunities between a nonprofit and a foundation. Set aside one hour a month to identify opportunities and funding for your grantees or nonprofit peers.

NAME	INTRODUCTION THIS MONTH	INTRODUCTION NEXT MONTH	INTRODUCTION THE ONE AFTER
E.G. SMALLSVILLE FOOD BANK	SARAH @ X FDN	ROSHAN @ Y FDN	ALMA @ ABC CORP FDN

COMMIT TO BIG, BOLD, & BETTER

These exercises are all designed for nonprofits and foundations to complete. You can do them on your own, but we encourage you to try them in a pair or group where both nonprofits and foundations are represented. These exercises will help you begin to think like partners—partners who want to think big, act boldly, and produce better results through all-in teamwork.

JOIN FORCES

Think about the miraculous feats of change and progress that we could create if we considered every other nonprofit and foundation as a partner in our vision—and saw ourselves as a partner in theirs.

Fill in your network of competitors, peers, funders, nonprofits, and other unicorn associates, but instead of your organization at the center, write your big bold common goal. So many people are working on that important goal!

OUR BIG COMMON GOAL IS:

YOUR ORG

How can you truly join forces with others you've listed on this page? Now identify three steps you can take to accelerate the goals and outcomes you're all working towards.

1.

2.

3.

SET ALL-IN EXPECTATIONS

Everyone does better when we know what to expect of each other in terms of communication. Charge your nonprofit or foundation team to discuss expectations for all involved at the outset of an EPIC Partnership.

Foundations: don't leave a nonprofit hanging, unable to plan for the future. Make it a habit and make it easy for nonprofits to discuss mutual expectations from the outset of a grant. Nonprofits: encourage your team to prioritize transparent communication, especially when a challenge or delay comes up. Don't be afraid to initiate the conversation.

Help your team feel ready and confident by drafting prompts and discussing or role-playing them together.

DRAFT A PROMPT TO DISCUSS MUTUAL EXPECTATIONS AT THE OUTSET OF A GRANT:

_____

_____

WHAT CAN THEY EXPECT WHEN A CHALLENGE OR DELAY COMES UP FOR...

YOU?   THEM?

_____   _____

_____   _____

_____   _____

_____   _____

CHAMPION RESULTS

There's no better way to show your peers that you respect their work than to champion it!

Instead of trash-talking fellow nonprofits, champion their results by shouting about them from the rooftops of social media: sharing, liking, re-tweeting them far and wide. Instead of advancing your own individual funding philosophies and mechanisms, work together as foundations—sharing, adopting, and celebrating each other's lessons on how to be EPIC Partners.

This month, pick one of your peers and champion their results whenever you get chance. Pick another next month and do the same. Keep a running tally. Try to beat last month's score. Or, invite a peer to do the same for you and see who wins.

PEER: _____

CHAMPION TALLY
THIS MONTH

PEER: _____

CHAMPION TALLY
NEXT MONTH

THINK BIGGER, BOLDER,

Strategic plans. We write them; we live by them; we file them on a shelf. What we rarely do is read our partners' and peers' plans so we can support their goals, drive resources in their direction, team up when it makes sense to do so, and work towards collectively producing bigger, bolder results.

Start with a few trusted partners and peers (other foundations, nonprofits, change initiatives, government, and businesses) and start a shared folder online named after your collective 'One Day' vision, eg.: 'One Day All Youth Have Good Jobs', or 'One Day We'll Have a Healthy Planet'. Invite everyone to upload their strategic plans, or as much as they are comfortable sharing.

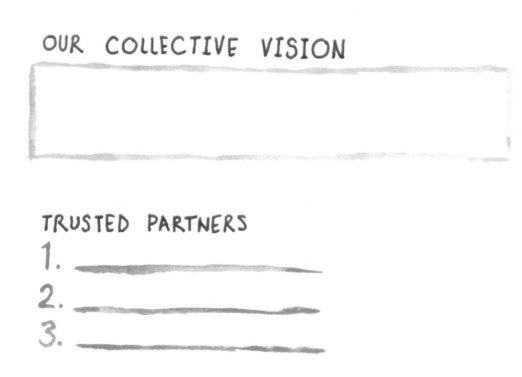

OUR COLLECTIVE VISION

TRUSTED PARTNERS
1. _____
2. _____
3. _____

AND BETTER TOGETHER

Encourage those partners and peers to invite others to join in, too.

Comment on each other's plans, flagging places where you can provide support, or where you could collaborate.

Challenge your assumptions around proprietary information. In the pursuit of vibrant communities and a healthy planet, does it matter who owns a solution when we all stand to benefit so greatly?

OTHERS TO INVITE

NP FDN

UNITE ALL UNICORNS

Nonprofits and foundations struggle to be in the same room as peers and teammates. Together, we could create better results—but only if we are all at the table, dreaming up bolder plans and exercising our all-in teamwork skills.

Dredge up the participant and speaker list from the last gathering, conference, roundtable, or convening you attended. Pull out the drawing of the Unicorn Family Tree (page 11).

Go through the participant and speaker list and make a tick mark next to the kind of unicorn on the tree that the participant is most closely identified with. Add some more of your own Unicorn Family member roles to the edges of the family tree, where needed, and tick these off, too.

Which members of the family were not represented at all? Which were under-represented? Which were over-represented?

Write an email (or an old-school handwritten letter) to the conference organizers to encourage them to include more branches of the Unicorn Family in subsequent years.

OVER-REPRESENTED

UNDER-REPRESENTED

NOT REPRESENTED

APPLAUD <u>TRUE</u> EPIC PARTNERSHIP

THANKS, XYZ FDN FOR GEN OPS $!
#EPICPARTNERSHIP

#UNICORNSUNITE

Thanks, to the nonprofit unicorns who advocated for our participation and voice at the table! #ALL-IN #EPICPARTNERSHIP
+57

When you see a unicorn adopting true EPIC Partnership, recognize and applaud the changes they are making! Change is rarely easy, and we all need encouragement as we advocate for new habits and practices in our organizations.

Don't fall into the trap of flattery-applause or vanity-ovations. We all like an ego boost, but those won't help us improve. If someone is window-dressing EPIC Partnership, keep walking. If someone is putting in hard work to truly shift mindsets and processes, then take a moment to give them feedback for doing a great job, show gratitude for how their changes positively affect your work, or simply show them a virtual thumbs up or high five!

So we can learn from and grow together, express your appreciation publicly whenever appropriate. Shout-out, post, tweet, blog, or selfie some unicorn love with hashtags!

#EPICpartnership

#UnicornsUnite

117

Then… once you've completed these exercises

the final step to make your unicorn dream come true

is to say the **magic words:**

ABRACADABRA!
OPEN SESAME!
MASHED POTATOES!

TA - DA!

Seriously, though…

IS THAT IT THEN?

If we all do these exercises will everything be perfect and peachy?

NOPE.

You'll have to figure it out as you go along.

This is just to get you started. It's all we had time for, as we all have full time jobs (and some of us have more than one). The important thing is, you're ready to start building real EPIC Partnerships, and to keep making them better over time.

Just don't forget...

YOU ARE NOT ALONE

Are you wondering if any of this will actually work? Of course, there's no money-back guarantee, but we've heard good things from organizations that have tried some of these exercises. For example:

We heard about a foundation that did the Baker's Dilemma exercise (page 96) during a board meeting. They recounted how, three minutes into the exercise, a board member suddenly exclaimed, "I get what this is demonstrating! This is why we should provide general operating support!" Success!

A nonprofit friend took some time to identify their priority needs, and then bravely started asking their funders for support to address them. It worked—and their funders began to help them with things that would help them take their work to the next level. Now they go in to every funder meeting with their top needs ready to courageously share. Success!

One foundation started sending handwritten thank-you notes after their meetings with their grantees. They heard back from several nonprofit unicorns that it was the first time a foundation unicorn had ever done that sort of thing—and that their simple expression of appreciation made the nonprofit unicorns feel valued for the work they do. This foundation's staff now love sending thank-you notes, as it helps to build appreciative relationships on an equal footing with the nonprofits they support. Success!

FEAR: WILL I FAIL?

RISK: MY BOARD WON'T GO FOR THIS...

We know it's not easy, and that you might be thinking…

STATUS: WHO WOULD LISTEN TO ME?

HABIT: WE CAN'T CHANGE...

CAPACITY: I DON'T HAVE TIME.

(Add your own concerns to this page!)

DOUBT: I'M ONLY ONE PERSON.

123

UNICORNS!
REPEAT AFTER ME !

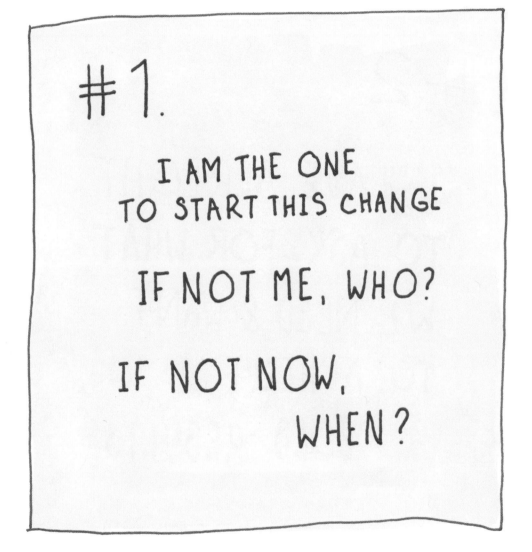

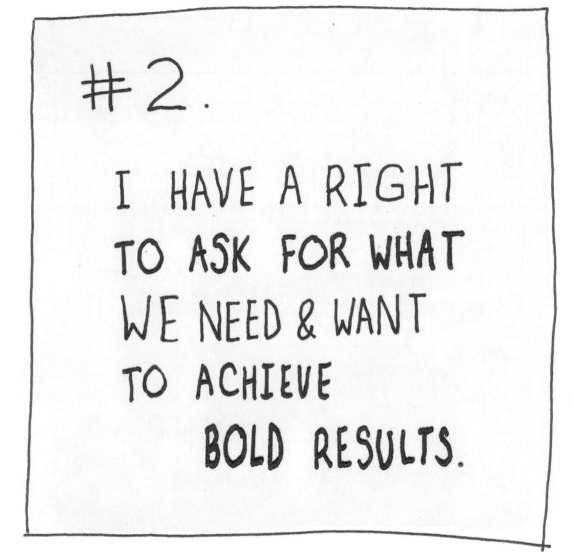

126

#3.

I HAVE POWER.
I HAVE INFLUENCE.
I CAN CREATE
EPIC PARTNERSHIPS.

WILL ONE PERSON'S ACTIONS CHANGE EVERYTHING

HMM... PROBABLY NOT, BUT...

IT ONLY TAKES THREE

TO START A PARTY!

THREE IN AN ORG

THREE ACROSS ORGS

THREE AT A CONFERENCE

THREE WRITING A BOOK!

GRAB  PICK

DO IT.

DISCUSS.

THE PLAN

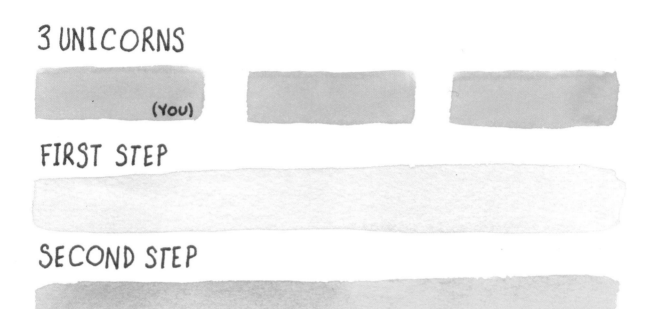

3 UNICORNS

(YOU)

FIRST STEP

SECOND STEP

WHAT WORKED

WHAT DIDN'T

IF YOU ONLY HAVE...

ONE HOUR PER MONTH, START HERE:

Value Inputs Beyond $	87
Value Time	88
Ask for What You Need	91
Nudge Your Needs	94
Ask Risky Questions	95
Dig Deeper	103
What Does it Take	104
Ask For Trust	106
Be an Advocate	109
Champion Results	113

Value Time	88
Anticipate Unknown Needs*	98
Identify Power Dynamics	102
What Does it Take*	104
Minimize the Power Dynamic	107
Be an Advocate	109

ONE HOUR PER YEAR START HERE:

Smash the Input Hierarchy	81
Look for What you Need	93
Put Client Needs First	99

Save Time	82
Reduce Due Diligence Time	84
Reduce Reporting Time	85
Align Time	86
Your Needs, Their Needs	92
The Number One Need*	96
Hire Empathy*	101

These are board-friendly exercises!

SHARE WHAT HAPPENS

When we share, we grow. Turn your party of three into a
party of more.

Grow your power, grow your influence, and grow your
impact by sharing your wild successes and blazing failures with your team, your board, and
your partners.

Continue the conversation by sharing at conferences,
meetings, online, in person, and through media of all kinds.

Share with us on the Unicorns Unite Facebook Group!
(facebook.com/UnicrnsUnite)

And don't forget to champion, encourage, and rejoice
with each other!

Let's do it.

We fight poverty and injustice. We restore and promote health and wellbeing.
We create and find jobs. We build housing. We educate children and train adults.
We preserve nature and wildlife. We secure human rights. We help everyone find their
power. We do hard, emotional, thoughtful, caring, challenging work every single day.

Build EPIC Partnerships? We are unicorns. We got this.

3, 2, 1,
UNICORNS
UNITE!

UNICORNS HUDDLE!

For additional resources and community tips
on how to build EPIC Partnerships,
or to sign and share the Unicorn Manifesto,
visit our Facebook page:

facebook.com/UnicrnsUnite

[remember to drop the 'o']

ACKNOWLEDGMENTS

Thanks to Josh Nesbit, Jocelyn Wyatt, Krista Donaldson for getting the ball rolling thinking about what nonprofits can do to exercise more power. Talking and brainstorming with you led us to writing this book.

Much appreciation to Vu's unicorn horde of NonprofitAF.com readers, who together adopted and embraced the term 'unicorn' for our field. You are our inspiration!

It was important to us that this book was representative of both the nonprofit and foundation perspectives, and that it was shaped and influenced by both. We are grateful to our many Kickstarter supporters (both nonprofit and foundation unicorns) and friends of unicorns from all over the country and the globe who put in the seed money to get this book off the ground. Because of their financial support, we were able to write and hone our message independently, not needing to rely on any one source of (potentially more directive) funding. We hope we represented our Kickstarter supporters' desire for a better unicorn future. Thank you for believing in us and the magic of our field, from the start!

The team over at Smarter Good was invaluable in the many ways they provided insights into the realities of fundraising and the experience of so many nonprofits and their foundation partners. Thank you for helping us make the book's nightmares more painfully real, and the dreams more grounded in hope.

So much love and appreciation to our amazing reviewers, who took time to read our drafts and help hone this book—it is bolder and better because of your ideas. A massive thanks to Rumsha Ahmed, Kriss Deiglmeier, Tory Dietel, Krista Donaldson, Christa Gannon, Dahna Goldstein, Carl Javier, Sue Johnson, Marina Kim, Sean Mayberry, and Christine Sherry.

We relied on a small elite force of get-shit-done ninjas: Elyse, Jocelyn, Sara, Alyssa, and Chiara. Thank you for the many hours of planning, organizing, herding, designing, and work you put in to help this book go from 'crazy idea' to 'real thing', over the past 18 months.

Where would we be without our editor, publisher extraordinaire, Katherine?!? We literally couldn't have done this without you. Thank you for helping us avoid writing someone else's book—and instead create this honest, fun, sometimes silly yet always uncompromising, imperfect little book of our own. It was truly a pleasure to do this with you.

Jessamyn and Vu, I always say that I'm too much of a control freak to be a co-founder. I am a new believer in the epic-ness of being a co-author. You made this project fun and provocative and do-able. I am your biggest fan and beyond grateful to the two of you. A huge thank you to the Smarter Gooders. Your daily work between foundation and nonprofit unicorns all over the globe and our ongoing conversations about how to create relationships that drive impact were the inspiration for this book. And to Ted, your support of decades of unicorn projects – mine, yours, and everyone's – is legendary. Thank you!

Love, Jane

Jane and Vu, When I grow up I want to be as bold and visionary as you, Jane, and as bravely outspoken and funny as you, Vu. Hoof high-fives all around, friends. Dave, thanks for taking a chance on me, showing me how to be a unicorn, and giving me the opportunity to build fun things filled with goodness. Much respect and many discoball emojis to the PF team for always striving to provide philanthropy with humanity and humility. Ali, thanks for keeping me laughing throughout this and the many other ridiculous ideas I come up with. You and the mooshes inspire my work and creations every single day :)

Love, Jessamyn

Jane and Jessamyn, Thank you for basically doing all of the work but still letting me feel like an actual co-author, like a real boy! It was intense, but I had a lot of fun and learned a bunch of important stuff working with you both. Stuff like unicorn puppetry, which will be handy for my next foundation site visit.

Love, Vu

Finally, we are grateful to you, our readers, the unicorns of our world.

Thank you for all that you do. Today, take a moment to give yourself some credit. You are a unicorn. A smart and charming and good-looking unicorn who is helping to make the world better. Take a moment to tell your colleagues that they are a unicorn to you.

Then, go home early and try not to work this weekend. Injustice and inequity will still be there to do battle with afterward. You deserve a break, you awesome unicorn you.

A BIG SHOUT OUT TO ALL THE UNICORNS

16 Amazing Anonymous Backers
Abby Arnold
Adam Naglich
Alexandra Bernadotte Nilsson
Aliza Dichter
Aliza Mazor
Allie Watson
Allison Levinsky
Allison M.
Amanda B. C. Paveglio
Amanda Card
Amy & John Rich
Amy J. Lenz
Ananda Valenzuela
Andrew Youn
Andy Perkins
Ann Corbett
Anna "Anya" Dausman
Anne Aaron
Anne Kirwan
Ava M. Rosenblatt
Avani Patel
Becca Katz
Becca Wammack
Ben Gong
Berit Ashla
Beth Kanter
Bethany Lister
Betsy Jones
Caitlyn Taylor
Carlin Johnson Politzer
Carol Metzger
Carole Kaiser Berwald
Caroli

Casey Allred
Catherine Casey
Charles Hoke
Cheryl Breuer
Christine Prentice Burton
Christy Remey Chin
Claire McDaniel
Claudia Bach
Conor Farese
Courtney A. Workman
Courtney Macavinta
Cynthia Foster
D Robillard
David Bornstein
David Kincheloe PhD MSW
David Rothschild
Dennis Peery
Edith Elliott, Noora Health
Elijah van der Giessen
Emily Zall
Erin Krampetz
Erin Okuno
Evan Hartsell
Everett Reiss
Farra Trompeter
Friends of Choice in Urban
Schools
Geoff A.
Gigi Naglak
Gracious Gamiao
Graham Snead
Guen Han
Heidi Neff
Henry Porter

Ingrid Haftel
Isabelle Moses
J McCray
Jacob Gong
Jamie Schumacher
Jana Byington-Smith
Jane Mitchell
Janet L. Rupp
Jason A. Weiner
Jean Gurney
Jen
Jennifer Lau
Jennifer Lynham Cunningham
Jennifer Simmons
Jennifer So Godzeno
Jennifer Sublett
Jess Main
Jessica Koscher
Jim Bildner
Jim Fruchterman
Joanne Schneider
Jocelyn Rheem
Jocelyn Wyatt
Jodi Doane
Jonathan C Lewis
Jordan Kassalow
Josh Nesbit
Judy Levine
Julia Kent
Julie Juergens
Kai Williams
Kalsada Coffee
Karen Kinney
Karen McCloskey

WHO SUPPORTED US ON KICKSTARTER!

Karen Nemsick
Karen Warr
Katherine B Ware
Kathryn Gilje
Kathy Heim
Kathy Kniep
Kathy Salmanowitz
Katy Ashe
💜 Krista Donaldson 💚
Lara Fox
Laura J. Heideman
Laura Perna
Lesley Matsa
Lewti Hunghanfoo
Liam O'Sullivan
LIN Center for Community
Development
Linda L. McDaniels
Linda Watkins
Lisa Kaylie
Liza J Dyer, CVA
Lori & Rose Fitzmaurice
Margaret Hall
Marilee Fenn
Marina Kim
Martha Bryant
Matthew Forti
Maura Teynor
Maureen Fitzgerald
Megan Brett
Meghan Kroning
Mira Wijayanti
Molly Wrobel Thompson
Nancy Farese

Nanette Fok
Naomi Baer
NetSuite.org
Nicholas Fusso
Nicole Levine
Pat Walsh
Patricia O'Brien
PEAK Grantmaking
Perla Ni
Peter Deitz
Renuka Kher
Rick Williams
Robin Mayasandra
Robin Wolaner
Rose Filicetti
Rose Green
Sabrina "Bowmanator" Bowman
Sallie Neillie
Sally Leu Naglich
Sam
Sam Vinal
Sara Jayne White
Sarah Clark
Sarah Cortell Vandersypen,
CFRE
Sarah P. Hanninen
Sarah Weintraub Schommer
Shannon Farley
Sharla Canning Wipplinger
Shira Saliman
Shoka Javadiangilani
Stephanie Dodson
StrongMinds
Tarah Evans

Taryn Goodman
Ted Levinson
Terry
Theresa Meyers
Tina Cincotti
Todd Manwaring
Tony Wang
Tracey A. Swanson
Tracey Weiss
Tracy Fischman
Travis Pitcher
Trisha Matthieu
Tyler Adams
Ursula Sandstrom
Valyrie K Laedlein
Vanessa Lau
Whitney H. Smith

THE AUTHORS

Jessamyn Shams-Lau

High school dropout turned MBA, Jessamyn currently co-creates and stewards the Peery Foundation's Grantee-Centric approach to philanthropy. Jessamyn is an advocate for interdisciplinary approaches, thoughtful risk taking, and bold ideas developed through apprenticing with a problem.

Jessamyn joined the Peery Foundation as its first non-family staff member in 2009, helping to shape the Foundation's initial approach and portfolios. Currently, as Executive Director, Jessamyn shapes and supports the Peery Foundation team, develops and guides overall strategy, and brings the Foundation Board's vision to life. Jessamyn utilizes her experience as part of the founding Ashoka U team in her hands-on role as a Board Member of BYU's Ballard Center, where she has created curriculum now taught at both the undergraduate and graduate levels. Jessamyn serves as an advisor to Ashoka U and GrantAdvisor.

Jessamyn has a BA in Fine Arts from the University of the Arts London and an MBA from Brigham Young University. She lives in the Bay Area with her ridiculously funny husband and two defiant house rabbits. You might also be interested to know that she used to have a mohawk haircut, she met her husband on Tinder, and her favourite (with a 'u', because she's British) Christmas film is *Die Hard 2*.

Jane Leu

An Ashoka Fellow, the Founder of Smarter Good, Upwardly Global and four other social sector start-ups, Jane Leu is intrigued by problems and their solutions. Known for strong vision and execution, Jane has more than twenty years of entrepreneurial leadership of social sector organizations.

Jane founded Smarter Good to help global social sector organizations start, sustain, and scale their impact. Smarter Good believes that by making a skilled team available to social sector innovators to support their fundraising, marketing and accounting and finance functions, they will have more time to focus on their missions, and that will lead to more global impact. With offices in the US and the Philippines, the Smarter Good team has worked at the intersection of hundreds of funders and more than 80 nonprofits working in 30 countries, across a diverse range of issue areas from youth development to poverty alleviation.

As the Founder and CEO of Upwardly Global, Jane built a national organization that has advanced the integration of thousands of skilled immigrant professionals into the workforce, turning the brain drain into brain gain for the US. Upwardly Global works closely with the private sector to connect employers, from multinational corporations to small businesses, to the benefits of a globally diverse workforce.

Jane is a Lecturer in Social Innovation at the Stanford Graduate School of Business, helping MBAs find their place in the social impact sector. She is a Draper Richards Kaplan Foundation Venture Partner, a member of the Board of Directors of Welcoming America, and an advisory board member of Ashoka U, and the Peery Foundation. Jane's contributions and leadership have been recognized by BYU Social Innovator of the Year Award, John F. Kennedy New Frontier Award, Draper Richards Kaplan Foundation for Social Entrepreneurship and the Manhattan Institute Social Entrepreneur Award, among others. She holds a MA from Columbia University's School of International and Public Affairs and a BA from Tufts University.

Lesser-known facts about Jane include: she spends a lot of happy hours talking to her dog, she never cooks, and as a legacy of her Midwestern roots, she would eat entire meals comprised only of corn-on-the-cob if it was deemed socially acceptable.

Vu Le (pronounced 'voo lay')

Vu is a writer, speaker, vegan, Pisces, and the Executive Director of Rainier Valley Corps—a nonprofit in Seattle that fosters social justice by developing leaders of color, strengthening organizations led by communities of color, and fostering collaboration between diverse communities.

Vu's passion to make the world better (combined with a low score on the Law School Admission Test) drove him into the field of nonprofit work, where he learned that we should take the work seriously, but not ourselves. There's tons of humor in the nonprofit world, and someone needs to document it. He is going to do that, with the hope that one day, a TV producer will see how cool and interesting our field is, and make a primetime show about nonprofit work—featuring attractive actors attending strategic planning meetings and filing 990 tax forms.

Known for his no-BS approach, irreverent sense of humor, and love of unicorns, Vu has been featured in dozens, if not hundreds, of his own blog posts at nonprofitAF.com. In his free time, Vu watches way too much TV (*Game of Thrones, Breaking Bad, 30Rock, Arrested Development, The Golden Girls*), and spends time with his spouse and kids during the commercial breaks.

UNICORN NOTES, IDEAS, DREAMS,

Red Press Ltd.
Unicorns Unite: How nonprofits and foundations can build EPIC Partnerships
Jessamyn Shams-Lau, Jane Leu, Vu Le

This is a work of nonfiction. Any resemblance to actual unicorns is not a coincidence.
No jargon was harmed in the making of this book.

Illustrated by Jessamyn Shams-Lau
Typeset in Amasis and Special Elite

Published by Red Press
ISBN 978 1 912157 04 4 (Paperback)
ISBN 978 1 912157 05 1 (Digital)

A catalogue record for this book is available from the British Library

Red Press Registered Offices:
6 Courtenay Close, Wareham, Dorset, BH20 4ED, England, Great Britain

Printed and bound at Thomson-Shore, USA on paper with 30% post-consumer recycled content.

www.redpress.co.uk
@redpresspub